The UPPER GLENKENS

by
Jack Hunter

The conservative character of the Glenkens, certainly in the matter of building techniques, is shown on this postcard, entitled 'Knowehead, near Dalry'. In 1792 local man Robert Heron commented that most of the houses in Dalry had thatched roofs, and that form of roofing was obviously still in use in the area in the early twentieth century. The latticework of poles used to secure the thatch suggests that Knowehead lived up to its name by occupying a very exposed position.

© Jack Hunter 2001
First published in the United Kingdom, 2001,
by Stenlake Publishing
Telephone / Fax: 01290 551122

ISBN 1 84033 160 7

FURTHER READING

In compiling this publication I have referred to many earlier works on the area, most of them long out of print. The main ones are listed here, while others are mentioned in the text. I am happy to acknowledge my indebtedness to all the authors whose books I have consulted. Please note that none of the following titles is available from Stenlake Publishing.

Dick, C. H., *Highways and Byways in Galloway and Carrick*
Gibson, Jean, *Around Dalry*
Gifford, John, *The Buildings of Scotland: Dumfries and Galloway*
Harper, Malcolm, *Rambles in Galloway*, second edition
Hill, George, *Tunnel and Dam – The Story of the Galloway Hydros*
M'Conchie, Wm., *Tours in Galloway*, 1907 and 1915 editions
M'Kerlie, P. H., *History of the Lands and Their Owners in Galloway*
Maxwell, J. H., *Maxwell's Guide Book to the Stewartry of Kirkcudbright*, eighth edition
Pigot & Slater, *Commercial Directories of Dumfries and Galloway*
Trotter, Alex., *East Galloway Sketches*
The Statistical Account of Scotland
The New Statistical Account of Scotland

ACKNOWLEDGEMENTS

In addition to the printed sources listed, I also have to thank Mr and Mrs Muir, New Galloway, for information. However, any factual errors and all opinions and conclusions are solely my responsibility.

On the Deugh near Dalshangan

Dalshangan, on the Deugh just before its confluence with the Ken, was for some years the home of Alexander Trotter, member of a notable Glenkens family and author of *East Galloway Sketches*, a treasure house of information about the Stewartry in general and the Glenkens in particular. At an earlier time it was another local property owned by Grier of Lag, so much detested for his anti-Covenanting activities (see page 28). Trees and rocky gorges were characteristic of the old Deugh–Ken riverscape prior to implementation of the hydroelectric scheme, which raised water levels considerably and left much of this scene submerged.

INTRODUCTION

The four parishes occupying the valley of the River Ken have been collectively known as the Glenkens for over 600 years: fourteenth century documents refer to 'the new forest of Glen Ken' (and suggest that some of the inhabitants were slaves). The present publication presumptuously dares to split the four, dealing only with Carsphairn, Dalry, Balmaclellan, and the northern part of Kells, coining for this new grouping the term 'Upper Glenkens'. The reasons for this affront to tradition are admittedly primarily practical; most of Kells parish fits conveniently with Parton, Crossmichael, and Balmaghie to provide material for a second, complementary book, *The Ken Valley*. However the geography of the area provides some justification for the split. This book ends at the Ken Bridge and thus very close to the point where the river broadens out and changes its name, along with its nature, to Loch Ken. Our Upper Glenkens therefore comprises those districts which border the river rather than the loch of the same name.

Besides, boundaries in the Glenkens, at least ecclesiastical ones, have never been sacrosanct. While the claim that the whole area was originally one parish is disputed, there is no doubt that around 1640 a new parish, Carsphairn, was created by removing a portion each from the parishes of Kells and Dalry.

Arguably the three outstanding characteristics of the Upper Glenkens are its conservative (with a small 'c'!) nature, its historical role as a stronghold of the Covenanting cause, and its physical transformation by one of Scotland's earliest hydroelectric projects.

The area's preference for the customary and the traditional may perhaps be a consequence of its geographical isolation. The trait could be seen, according to S. R. Crockett, in the speech of the inhabitants: 'it is indeed only towards the fastnesses of the Dungeon of Buchan and the butts of Millyae that one finds the true, unalloyed speech of Galloway . . . the actual and ancient speech of the Free Province'. Contemporary historian Innes Macleod believes this may have been one of the last places in Galloway where Gaelic was spoken, as late as the seventeenth century. The same conservative tendency may have operated in agriculture. Pigot & Co.'s *Commercial Directory* for 1825–1826 claimed that the Glenkens were famous for the true, native breeds of cattle, sheep, and horses at a time when the last two of those would have disappeared from much of Galloway.

However, the conservatism of the area showed less happily in the persistence to the end of the seventeenth century at least of the belief that the Devil and his agents were physically present and active in the community. Thus in 1677 the Carsphairn minister ordered his parishioners not to assist a black-clad stranger in danger of drowning while trying to cross the flooded

Deugh on the grounds that he was the Devil. And in 1698 an old woman, Elspeth MacEwan, from Bogha' near Balmaclellan, was accused of witchcraft and hauled off to be burnt at the stake at Kirkcudbright.

Whether because of conservatism, geographical isolation, or other cause, the Upper Glenkens was certainly a bastion of the Covenanting interest in the political/religious troubles which tormented Scotland in the second half of the seventeenth century; one of the most serious challenges to government authority, the Pentland Rising of 1666, began in Dalry. The determination of the authorities to remove all opposition to Episcopalianism was matched by the Presbyterian resolution to maintain their traditional forms of worship and church government. Neither side had a monopoly of virtue or excess. The killing of the Episcopalian minister of Carsphairn in his own manse was matched by the torture of Mrs MacGill of Balmaclellan in frustration at the soldiers' failure to capture her husband – treatment which led to her death. It is difficult to disagree with the assessment of Scott's Wandering Willie: 'Wild wark they made of it; for the Whigs (Covenanters) were as dour as the Cavaliers were fierce'. Presbyterianism triumphed with the 1688 Revolution and the fall of the Stewarts (although some Presbyterians did not think so) and has also been victorious in the propaganda war since.

For a conservative area the construction of the Galloway hydroelectric scheme in the 1930s must have been a considerable shock. The enterprise was conceived by three Stewartry residents, Messrs Wellwood Maxwell, Scott Elliot, and William McLellan, the latter being the prime mover as director of a firm of electrical engineering consultants. They saw the potential afforded by the terrain and rainfall of the north of Kirkcudbrightshire. Work began on the £3 million scheme in 1931 and was completed in 1936. The design incorporated three storage reservoirs: the natural Lochs Doon and Ken and the artificial Clatteringshaws Loch, formed by damming the Black Water of Dee, a western tributary of the Ken.

The project was an imaginative and ingenious one. The natural outlet northwards of Loch Doon was dammed and a tunnel built to divert its water southwards via the Carsphairn Lane into the Deugh–Ken river system. By reversing the flow in the tunnel, surplus water from the Deugh and its tributaries could be stored in Loch Doon till required. Most ingenious of all, the same water was used to power the turbines in more than one station. Thus all the water driving the turbines at Tongland, the most southerly station, had already been used in at least one station upstream and some of it had been used three times.

It was not surprising that the construction of the Galloway Water Power

Scheme in an area of outstanding natural beauty aroused much hostile criticism, perhaps most forcefully and concisely put by a local poet:

> The company promoter's pen
> Will dam the Deugh and dam the Ken
> And dam the Dee – oh, damn the men
> Who plan such desecration!

On the other hand, the provision of an abundant supply of electricity at a special local rate was a huge benefit to the residents of the Stewartry. By 1960 almost all homes and farms in the county had an electricity supply. A 1960s photograph of Balmaclellan village ablaze with light reinforces the comment of the minister at that time that the domestic electrical appliances then available 'add to the comfort, health, and efficiency of the householders.'

The scheme was not, however, primarily for the benefit of local residents. Its main function was and remains to supply the national grid, providing the extra capacity needed at peak periods and utilising for this purpose the very short start-up time required by hydro stations. These latter by their presence in the landscape are a reminder of the enormous range in time covered by human activity in this secluded, lovely part of Galloway.

The Bruce's Stone on Moss Raploch, near New Galloway.

Left: In 1307 the Clatteringshaws area was the scene of a skirmish between Robert the Bruce, then a fugitive in the Galloway hills, and a pursuing English force. With greatly inferior numbers, Bruce took local advice and gathered together all the horses, wild and domesticated, and goats in the district and kept the herd within sound but out of sight of the English troops. The resultant noise and the appearance of the animals on the skyline in the uncertain light of dusk convinced his foes that they were opposed by a vastly superior force, and when the Scots attacked at dawn they easily put the English to flight, giving Bruce an important psychological victory. The King's Stone, the boulder against which he allegedly rested at the close of the fight, stands today on the north-east shore of Clatteringshaws Loch, the artificial loch created as part of the Galloway Water Power Scheme. The official history of the power scheme, George Hill's *Tunnel and Dam*, claims this is the stone's original location, but C. H. Dick states that it had to be moved when the reservoir was created.

Carsphairn & the Carrick Hills, Kirkcudbrightshire.

A. 2180.

The village of Carsphairn, spelled in earlier times Carsefairn or Carsefern, dates from the late eighteenth century, when it contained 60 inhabitants. Its Gaelic name, meaning 'the wet ground of the alders', is appropriate since it is situated on the bed of a former loch. According to a former incumbent, the parish church (the present version of which was built around 1815 and is prominent on the left) was built on a sandbank of that loch – in clear contravention of biblical teaching. The treeless moorlands and bare hills of the surrounding countryside, much commented on by earlier writers, are very obvious here; Forestry Commission planting in recent years has added the ubiquitous conifer to the scene. Scattered over the hillside in the right background are the buildings of the Woodhead mine (see page 10), whose workforce necessitated the building of a gallery in the church for their accommodation. Both workforce and gallery have long gone.

Belying the peacefulness of this main street scene looking north, Carsphairn in 1905 boasted a blacksmith, two bootmakers, a draper, two grocers, a joiner, a spirit dealer, and a tailor, indicating a degree of self-sufficiency necessary in this most northerly settlement in the Stewartry, which snow frequently left cut off even in the 1960s. Had things worked out differently, the village might have had even more facilities to offer. In 1672 a local laird, the notorious Grier of Lag, whose family had long owned the Garryhorn estate, was granted a charter to create a burgh of barony at the Kirktoun of Carsphairn, with a provost, bailies, a tolbooth, a cross, a weekly market, and two fairs yearly. Sadly the charter was never implemented.

The Salutation Hotel, now converted into flats, was the largest building in Carsphairn and one of the village's principal landmarks. Rebuilt and enlarged around 1900, it had added a Shell petrol pump to its other facilities by the time of this picture. The hotel seems to have had a chequered career, at periods being closed down. It was fully functional in 1908, however, when proprietrix Mrs Mitchell declared the establishment was 'replete with every modern convenience' and offered posting (horse-drawn transport for hire) in all its branches with the assurance of careful drivers. The impressive size of the hotel may have been deceptive; by the 1950s it advertised only eight letting bedrooms.

The Sheep, Carsphairn.

The takeover by sheep of Carsphairn main street seems entirely appropriate, for sheep farming has always been the parish's economic mainstay, apart from a brief period when the Woodhead lead mines flourished. A nineteenth century writer put it graphically but succinctly, saying sheep were what farmers depended on 'for necessities, for comfort, and for riches'. At that time the sheep reared were Blackfaced, efforts to introduce whitefaced breeds having been unsuccessful. Part of the area's suitability for sheep farming lies in the fact, we are told, that the hills are green right to the tops. This may explain the fact that in 1792 the parish supported 30,000 sheep, most flocks being 2,000 strong. By the early twentieth century it was claimed that 30,000 sheep were reared annually, with the Cheviot breed having joined the Blackfaced as the main type. A joiner and cartwright's business appears to occupy the premises in the left foreground.

Sheep dipping, Carsphairn. Given the economic importance of sheep rearing, dipping would have been a very important occasion. An eighteenth century writer gives an alarming account of sheep diseases prevalent in the area; these included the dauntingly-named gripping, hydrocephalus, and vanquish, the last-named being particularly appropriate because it was almost always fatal after clearly identifying its victims by turning their horns red.

As in many Scottish congregations, numbers of Carsphairn churchgoers broke away from the Church of Scotland at the Disruption of 1843 to join the newly created Free Church – later United Free Church – of Scotland. By 1916 the UF minister in the parish was the Revd C. H. Dick, author of the classic work *Highways and Byways in Galloway and Carrick*. Dick was a friend from university days of the better-known author John Buchan, who came to Carsphairn to hear him take his first service and afterwards treated him to lunch in the Salutation Hotel. The bicycle parked behind the railings on the left raises the tantalising possibility that the gentleman at the gate of Carsphairn UF manse might be Dick himself, for the minister was, like Buchan, an enthusiastic cyclist. Indeed it was numerous cycling trips made the length and breadth of Galloway and beyond, using a specially designed bicycle, which gave Dick his intimate and unrivalled knowledge of the area.

Woodhead Lead Mines, Carsphairn.

Lead, with some copper and zinc and a little silver, was discovered in 1838 on the slopes of Coran of Portmark 'in the bosom of a remote mountain' just west of Carsphairn. Mining began soon afterwards. By the mid-1840s the mines were in full production with more than ten vertical shafts, crushing equipment powered by a 30-foot water wheel (visible in the picture), and smelting furnaces. The bars of processed lead were taken to Ayr for shipment to Liverpool. A large village with a population of 300 was built beside the mines to accommodate workers and their families, who mostly came from Leadhills and Wanlockhead. The village possessed a two-teacher school while the estate- and mines owner, Colonel Macadam, also contributed a library. During the operation's heyday it was claimed that more money circulated in a week in the parish than had previously done so in a year. However, the good times did not last. By the 1870s the village population had dropped to 100 inhabitants, mainly from Cornwall, and the mines were leased out to a Scotsman named Campbell. The enterprise had been abandoned by around 1890.

LAGWYNE CASTLE, CARSPHAIRN   249

Lagwine 'Castle', north of Carsphairn, was built in the early eighteenth century as a new residence for a prominent local family, the Macadams of Waterhead. John Loudon Macadam, celebrated road engineer and inventor of the road surface that bears his name, was a member of this family. Sadly for local pride he was not born at Lagwine but in Ayr, where the family were temporarily staying at the time of his birth in September 1756. However, Lagwine was almost the scene of his demise a year later, when the house was destroyed by fire while the family were in residence. It was never rebuilt. The Macadams had to sell the Waterhead estate to pay debts incurred by the collapse of the Douglas and Heron (or Ayr) Bank, in which the laird was a shareholder.

Unveiling of Carsphairn War Memorial.

Carsphairn war memorial, lying just south of the village, was unveiled in 1923 by a distinguished native of the parish, Colonel Wm. H. Clark-Kennedy VC of Knockgray, who had served in the Canadian Army. He is probably the figure on the minister's immediate right. Coincidentally, another famous military figure from the First World War, who also served with the Canadian Army, had strong Carsphairn connections. Colonel John McCrae, author of that conflict's most famous poem, the celebrated *In Flanders Fields*, was the great-grandson of a parish resident, David McCrae, who emigrated with his family and grandchildren to Guelph in Canada in 1849. The memorial is built of local stone.

Carsphairn golf course was one of three in the Glenkens, the low ground beside the river south of the village offering a less searching test than the terrain of the Dalry and New Galloway courses. Built just before the First World War, it closed in 1946 after the Second World War had made its maintenance difficult. Unusually, it was located on the 18-acre glebe. Golfers had to share it with grazing sheep, although this was a normal arrangement on small, rural courses.

Silver Sands, Loch Enoch, Carsphairn

Lonely Loch Enoch, situated in the shadow of the Merrick on the border between Galloway and Ayrshire, is the highest body of water in Britain and the deepest loch in the south of Scotland. On its east side occur the famous silver sands, or silver strands; beaches of spectacularly white grains of eroded granite. Aside from its beauty, Loch Enoch sand was in great demand for sharpening scythes in the days when all mowing was done by hand. Because of the loch's remoteness, bringing back bags of this commodity must have been a long and exhausting task, which may explain the unenthusiastic expressions on the faces of the gentlemen in the picture. In Crockett's *The Raiders*, Silver Sand, who owes his nickname to his official occupation as an itinerant seller of scythe sand, waxes enthusiastic about the qualities of the Loch Enoch variety.

Knockgray, confusingly claimed to derive from the Gaelic 'hill of the elevated flat', lies just south of Carsphairn and is associated with the Clark-Kennedy family. In addition to the First World War winner of the Victoria Cross (see page 12), the family claims another military hero in Colonel Alexander Clark-Kennedy of the Royal Dragoons, who personally captured the eagle and colours of a French regiment at the Battle of Waterloo. The late nineteenth century laird of the same family was distinguished in a different way. A poet, naturalist, and field sportsman, he transformed the moorland hillside round the former shooting lodge into 'a garden in a wilderness' by judicious planting of fine trees and shrubs.

The present Knocknalling mansion house was built by John Kennedy (1769–1855). According to Glenkens tradition, he was one of four local men who among them founded the Lancashire cotton spinning industry. Certainly Kennedy was a major figure in this industry. A member of a branch of the famous Ayrshire Kennedies, which claimed to have owned the property since the fifteenth century, he was born into straitened circumstances. Having learned the trade of carpentry, he moved south to join a firm near Manchester which was owned by a Glenkens man. There he made machinery for the infant cotton industry. He later branched out to set up a separate business with another local man, and then diversified into cotton spinning, eventually owning several mills. In later life he spent his summers at Knocknalling and planned to establish a cotton mill on the Ken at nearby Allangibbon Bridge. Unfortunately for the local economy, the plan came to nothing, although some preliminary work was done.

The distinctive humpbacked shape of Cairnsmore of Carsphairn is visible from much of the Ken valley. Its pre-eminence among the three Galloway Cairnsmores is recognised in the old rhyme:

> There's Cairnsmore of Fleet and Cairnsmore o' Dee,
> And Cairnsmore of Carsphairn, the highest o' the three.

It was one of the hills which so impressed noted Scottish judge and author Lord Cockburn on his first visit to the Carsphairn area as 'real, plainly marked, sticking-up mountains'. Local tradition asserts that some of the streams rising on this Cairnsmore contain alluvial gold, and that an enterprising Dr Dodds once collected it with 'paper-mills' and then set up a workplace where he minted the gold into doubloons. When the authorities showed an unsympathetic interest in his activities, he threw his equipment into the Green Well of Lagwine and escaped legal retribution.

Earlston Castle, Dalry

This late sixteenth century L-shaped tower house north of Dalry is associated with one of Galloway's most famous families. The estate and castle were obtained by a branch of the Gordons of Lochinvar in 1601. During the troubles of the second half of the seventeenth century the Gordons of Earlstoun were leading supporters of the Covenanting cause, none more so than Alexander Gordon, known as 'The Bull of Earlstoun' because of his strength. Fined, outlawed, his estate forfeited, he was eventually captured, but before being executed was brought before the Privy Council in Edinburgh for torture to obtain information. An enraged 'Bull' then broke his chains, overpowered his guards, escaped from his cage, and put to undignified flight a terrified Privy Council. Declared insane and imprisoned on the Bass Rock, he was freed and restored to his estates at the Revolution of 1688. Alexander and the castle appear in Crockett's novels, along with other members of the Gordon family.

DALRY FROM WATERSIDE HILL

The traveller on the Ayr to Castle Douglas road (middle of picture, left to right) gets a false impression of the size of Dalry. Most of the village in fact lies on the Old Edinburgh Road running down the hillside to the fords across the River Ken. The setting of a traditional Glenkens tale, which inspired Burns's *Tam o' Shanter*, is clearly visible. Adam Forrester of Knocksheen, returning home from a visit to the Midtown Inn in Dalry, disturbed a gathering of witches and warlocks in the church (on the site of the modern version, centre right). Hotly pursued, he crossed the Ken and the meadow beyond and then fled up the now wooded slopes of Waterside Hill (foreground). With the pursuit closing, he dismounted and made a circle with his sword in the turf. He blessed the circle, making it holy ground, and then sought refuge with his horse inside it. The stratagem worked, but only after the terrified horse had backed outside the very restricted safe area and had its tail pulled off.

The impressive size of the Lochinvar Hotel (30 rooms in 1915) is a reminder that for a time from the end of the nineteenth century Dalry was a very popular holiday resort, particularly for health reasons. A contemporary writer commented that in summer and autumn the village was crowded with visitors; another writer noted with approval that these visitors were of the kind who could amuse themselves. The croquet lawn with its own pavilion was obviously one of the more elegant recreations. Lochinvar Hotel and its neighbours at the foot of the hill on the Ayr to Castle Douglas road are in the newest part of the village. Newfield farm – situated somewhat incongruously across the road from the hotel – would originally have been surrounded by fields.

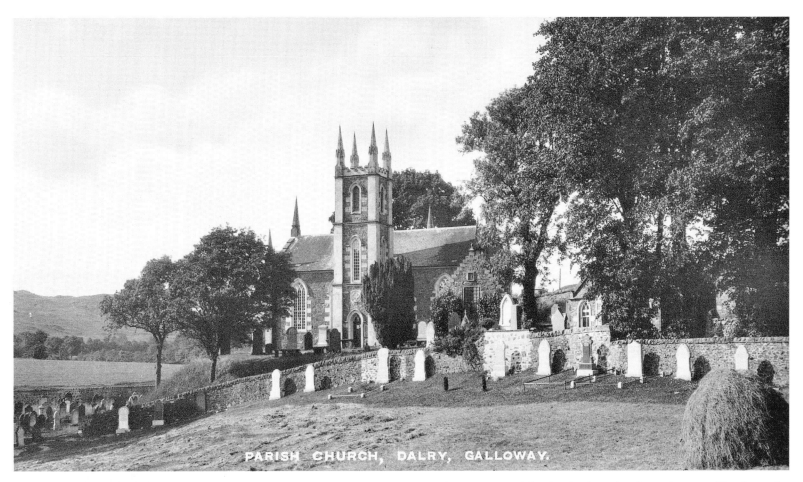

PARISH CHURCH, DALRY, GALLOWAY.

Just to the right of centre of this picture of Dalry church, the crow-stepped gable of the remains of the Gordon burial aisle can be seen. This bears the date 1546 and forms part of the old Dalry kirk, where Adam Forrester, prototype of Tam o' Shanter, encountered 'the hellish legion' at their revels. The gable window is covered by an unusual iron grille and above it are the combined arms of the Gordon and Crichton families. In the sixteenth century this old kirk was the scene of a strange tragedy. A son had been born to the Sinclair family, who owned Earlstoun before the Gordons, and it had been prophesied that he would be drowned on his seventh birthday. On that occasion, a Sunday, his mother took him to Dalry kirk, well away from the dangers of the Ken. On her arrival she stopped to speak to friends and the child wandered off. When she went to search for him she found him drowned in the baptismal font.

The junction of Main Street and the Ayr road is the focal point of Dalry's New Town. The church-like building (which has a red-tiled steeple) is, in fact, the town hall. To the left, the dairy and Commercial Hotel buildings have today been combined to form the Clachan Inn. Rankin & Sons' bakery on the right is now a private house. In the centre of the street is the Cross or McNaught's Fountain, erected in 1917 as a gift to the community from a grocer and general merchant in the village. The fountain, intended for the refreshment of horses, no longer runs and the lamp has gone from the top. The lamp bracket on the corner of the dairy is a reminder that Dalry had street lighting from early in the twentieth century, originally provided by oil lamps. In 1926 an Electricity Supply Company was set up with 21 subscribers to provide both domestic supplies and 11 street lights. With the advent of the hydroelectric scheme it was bought over by the county council.

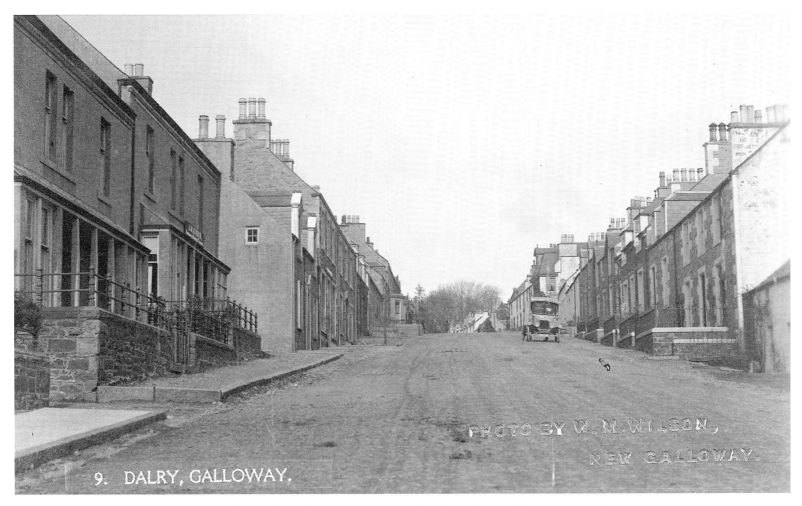

9. DALRY, GALLOWAY.

PHOTO BY W. M. WILSON, NEW GALLOWAY.

Main Street links the site of the church with the older village further up the hill. Most of its buildings date from the late eighteenth century when the Earl of Galloway, then owner of the land, feued ground for houses here. The domestic exteriors hide a variety of former uses. The house on the left, for instance, with the small window in the gable, is the old court house. It was here that a mob of angry villagers besieged the local magistrates at the end of the eighteenth century when the latter tried to implement a law on conscription into the militia, forcing them to flee by the back door. The low house partly visible on the right may be the former smithy, the upper room of which was used as a Roman Catholic chapel. Also on the right is a former inn.

Dalry, Galloway.

The main reason for Dalry's popularity as a holiday resort in pictorial form: its splendid situation looking across the Ken valley to the hills on the western side and, not shown here, the magnificent Rhinns of Kells range. The abundance of flowers and climbers luxuriating on the house fronts and the pure, bracing, upland air, the consequence of its elevated situation, were also among Dalry's attractions. However, one guidebook's description of the village as 'The Galloway Sanatorium' was not perhaps the happiest way of couching the advantage of its fresh air. On the left may be seen one of the Electricity Supply Company's street lights.

Dalry Galloway 18.

The Gordon Hotel at the top of Main Street displays the typical Dalry feature of an abundance of climbing plants on its frontage. The hotel was one of two 'dry' establishments in the village, the other being the Temperance Refreshment Room; evidence that the great temperance movement of the nineteenth and early twentieth centuries in Scotland had reached the Glenkens. Like the Lochinvar, the Gordon Hotel was enlarged to meet the tourist boom, with a new 'dining hall' and lounge being added just before the Great War, an unfortunate piece of timing. A satisfied customer of the day commended the hotel for its dainty service, combined with moderate charges. Today the building is private residences.

ROTCHEL TERRACE, DALRY

Rotchel Terrace, situated above Main Street, marks the start of the old part of Dalry. This is reflected in its name, which formerly applied to the area and may derive from 'La Rochelle' (the Little Rock) – possibly the name of a medieval hospice for pilgrims on the road from Edinburgh to Scotland's most important place of pilgrimage, the shrine of St Ninian at Whithorn. Whithorn was frequently visited by King James IV, who occasionally travelled by this route. The Lord High Treasurer's accounts reassure us that the king did not spurn Dalry's hospitality, containing as they do several entries for 'belchair', the appropriate Old Scots word for bed and breakfast. The ground behind the wall on the left, now the policies of a mansion, was formerly known as Knockcardie, Gaelic for 'the tinkers' knowe', as this was the place where travelling people pitched their tents.

276/14

Despite its name Midtown is the oldest part of Dalry, and some of the renovated houses may date back 400 years. The Midtown Inn, where the incident that triggered the Pentland Rising of 1666 began, and where Adam Forrester had been on the night of his brush with the Dalry witches, stood here until the late nineteenth century. Beyond the house on the left with its gable to the street is the wall surrounding the wooded ground of the former Knockcardie. Here, where the street levels out, was the district of Underhill, lying between Midtown and Rotchel. While its name appears quite appropriate from this vantage point, it seems perhaps less so to visitors climbing up the Main Street from the Cross.

Creganfois, Dalry

JV 54705

Situated just outside Dalry to the north-east, Creaganfois was originally the Old Free Grammar Schoolhouse, comprising school and master's house. Built around 1760, it was the second building to serve as Free Grammar School, the original having been at Underhill. Founded in 1668 with a bequest of £1,000, the school was unusual in offering free education and acquired a high academic reputation that brought pupils from a distance. By 1900 the school had closed and the building was being used as a private residence. In the 1930s Creaganfois was owned by Mr R. Curtis-Hayward, an artist. An unusual small building of brick and corrugated iron in the grounds may have been his studio.

Situated close to Creaganfois, Mossrodick (or Mossroddock) is one of the lochs that made this area highly popular with anglers. The fish populating it seem, however, to have been unusual. Large, brilliantly coloured, and with rich pink flesh, the trout were rarely caught. More remarkably, one writer claimed that the Mossrodick fish, actually few in number, deliberately moved rapidly round the loch to give the impression that it was alive with trout. In winter the local club used the loch for curling. In summer it was a favourite resort of the author C. H. Dick because of its quietness and solitude.

Neil Gunn, the famous Scottish novelist, lived for two years in Dalry in his early teens, staying with his married sister. One of his great pleasures was playing golf on the 9-hole course, which was close to his sister's house. He describes golf at Dalry as 'a half-visible game full of alpine surprises', explaining that although the holes were short the green could rarely be seen from the tee and then only from a height. However, he applied the principles of Zen philosophy to his golf to good effect, equalling the course record of 33. A brilliant literary career was almost destroyed when he was partnering a powerfully-built lady. Going forward from the tee to mark her ball but prudently keeping well off the line of the drive, he was felled by a powerful but errant shot which struck him on the forehead.

KEN VALLEY FROM GOLF COURSE, DALRY.

Since parts of the Ken–Deugh catchment area have an annual rainfall in excess of 60 inches, flooding along the river was a frequent problem, as the embankments in this picture, entitled 'Glenlee road in flood, Dalry', prove. In 1840 a local minister recorded that the valley was like an inland sea after the frequent inundations. The worst time for floods, he said, was the end of July and early August, the period of 'the Lammas spate'. One length of flood embankment is visible on the far bank to the left of the tree. It is claimed locally that some parts of those barriers were built by French prisoners of war during the Napoleonic Wars.

Although the road – from Dalry to New Galloway on the west bank of the Ken – is the same as that in the picture above, the two views offer a complete contrast in every other respect. Hay from the meadows along the Ken was a very important element in the scheme of things in this part of the Glenkens, and the load being carted to the farm would have gladdened the farmer's heart. It has been suggested that the silt from the flooded Ken contributed materially to the fertility of the river meadows.

Situated in the glen of that name on the other side of the river from Dalry, Old Garroch House was formerly known as Ballingear. Its Gaelic name, meaning 'rough land', was certainly apt during the troubles of the late seventeenth century, when it was used as a base by the Covenanters' arch-foe, Grier of Lag. However one fugitive had cause to bless it. William Stevenson of Barbeth, having been captured and his hands and feet bound with raw hide (in the absence of rope), was thrown into a Garroch outhouse overnight prior to torture and execution. During the night he was visited by rats which providentially nibbled at his bonds, thus allowing him to free himself. With the door barred he escaped by making a hole in the roof thatch. In the morning he was hotly pursued by a 'red-wudd-ragin' Grier but made his escape.

A 'considerable house' existed at Glenlee, near Old Garroch, as early as 1684. In the eighteenth and nineteenth centuries it was owned by a notable legal family, the Millers, a father and son of which both became Lords of Session. Another member of the family was 'turkey Jock Miller . . . the famous fat laird', a man of prodigious appetite. The house is reputed to have two ghosts. The Grey Lady is the shade of a Lady Ashburton, who, according to your preference, either poisoned her husband or was poisoned by the butler for her valuables. The presence of another ghost was revealed when a guest examining a photograph album remarked that he recognised an elderly gentleman, as the latter had entered his bedroom in error that morning. He was told that the subject of the photo had been dead for many years.

The view of Balmaclellan from the top of the motte reveals its street plan as an ornately drawn 'J'. The stem or leg of the 'J' in the foreground runs up towards the war memorial. The crosspiece to the left climbs towards a junction with the Corsock to Ken Bridge road and on the right curls towards the church and the western exit from the village. The centre of the picture boasts as yet no filling station, while the gable of the large building beyond features a second-storey window and a clock, both of which have now disappeared. Bennan Hill on the far side of Loch Ken is prominent in the right background. The village takes its name, once again of Gaelic origin, from one John Maclellan, a member of an extensive and prominent Stewartry family, who in 1466 obtained the land in this area; hence 'the village of Maclellan'. The claim that the village was formerly known as The Casa lacks evidence.

1. BALMACLELLAN.

PHOTO BY W. M. WILSON, NEW GALLOWAY.

The road from the centre of Balmaclellan east to the war memorial appears undeveloped here without the village hall, built in 1919, and the four steel and roughcast council houses of 1949. While the village lies in a depression, the view from the surrounding higher ground of the Ken valley to the north is magnificent. The Balmaclellan area is noted for its large number of drumlins; small, whale-backed hills, the result of glaciation.

In the days before the car and tractor the village blacksmith was a key figure in the rural community, and Balmaclellan possessed two smithies. The cart in the centre of the picture is a reminder of the other essential rural craftsman, the joiner. In the mid-nineteenth century the village's joiner was Peter Gordon. Another contemporary craftsman was millwright James M'Queen, whose skills would have been welcomed by the numerous mills in the parish. The gentlemen in the foreground exemplify the parish minister's comments in 1792 about the character of the inhabitants: peaceful and sober but with the necessary spirit on occasion to assert their rights. Like neighbouring Dalry, the village obviously had some form of street lighting.

The smithy, the whitewashed building on the far right, eventually moved down the street to occupy the premises on the extreme left, still used today by its successor, an agricultural engineer's business. Both smithy and engineering business have been run for generations by the same family, the Corries. The previous smithy has today shed its whitewashed exterior in favour of the original local stone and is a private house. The building on its left was a community library founded in 1878 by William Barbour of Barlay, as the plaque above the door attests. The mound in the background shaped like an upturned plum pudding dates from the late twelfth century. Known as a motte, it was the base for a wooden castle erected by an Anglo–Norman nobleman who was given land in the area by the king in return for keeping the local inhabitants in order. The original village would have sprung up beside the castle.

Balmaclellan.

The whitewashed buildings in the centre of the picture – and the centre of the village – have disappeared, but the church still dominates the scene. Originally built in 1753, it underwent various alterations, including one at the end of the nineteenth century when its large, square tower, celebrated in a local poem as 'Balmaclellan's stately tower', was removed. Some local critics felt the resulting building looked more like a villa than a church. C. H. Dick thought the village a delightful place lacking only one thing: accommodation for visitors. The situation is the same today as in 1916, with no inn or hotel. However, between the wars accommodation for members of a national cycling club was offered by one householder.

Balmaclellan Church.

The minister most prominently associated with Balmaclellan church is the Revd George Murray, who served here for much of the second half of the nineteenth century. A native of New Galloway and a keen sportsman, in his youth he sallied forth to Carsphairn races, took on and beat the local shepherds, and handed over his winnings to the parish poor. In later life he was an equally successful antiquarian, botanist, horticulturalist, agriculturalist, and poet. As a minister he founded a miniature dynasty, being succeeded by his son, who was in turn succeeded by his son-in-law. A strikingly-decorated memorial in the churchyard to five local men who died in the Crimean War provides a potted history of that conflict, listing Sebastopol, the Alma, Balaclava, Inkerman, Scutari hospital, and the assault on the Redan.

The best-known name connected with Balmaclellan was neither born there nor lived there, and isn't even buried there. Robert Paterson, a stonemason and native of Dumfriesshire, devoted most of his life to restoring and erecting Covenanters' memorials throughout Galloway. Eventually his wife, in the hope of seeing more of him, moved the family home to Balmaclellan in 1768, where she ran a small school to support herself and her children. She and others of the family are buried in the local churchyard. One of her sons, a lifelong resident of the village, in old age told antiquary Joseph Train of his father's vocation. Train relayed this to Sir Walter Scott, who introduced Paterson into his novel *Old Mortality*, giving him the name by which the world knows him. The statues, carved in 1840 by John Corrie of the famous blacksmithing family, stood for a long time in the grounds of the Holme estate. In 2000 they were re-erected in the churchyard overlooking the entrance to the village.

Old Mortality, Balmaclellan

KENTUCKY, BALMACLELLAN.   J. MITCHELL, NEW GALLOWAY.

The attractiveness of Kentucky cottage is as striking as its incongruous name. The securing of the thatch by ropes instead of poles and the eye-catching roof ridge indicate a much more sheltered position than the Knowehead cottages (page 1), a fact confirmed by the surrounding vegetation. In fact, the cottage stood at the junction of the western exit from Balmaclellan and the modern A769 to Bogue Toll. Sadly it has completely disappeared, but the site is marked by a seat inscribed 'Kentucky' set in a small, landscaped area.

Bogue or Glenkens Free Church, equidistant (and an inconvenient two miles) from Dalry and Balmaclellan, seems to have been set up to serve both communities after the Disruption of 1843. Its minister in 1852 was the Revd John Haining, at which time there was also a United Presbyterian chapel in Dalry. The union of the two sects in 1900 led to the building of a United Free Church in Dalry and the closure of the Bogue church. It was subsequently demolished and the lowest courses of its walls used to enclose part of the garden of the former manse, now a private house. The church had consisted of two long, narrow, unadorned buildings set side by side and linked, a design found elsewhere in Galloway.

Gordonston clachan and mill stood east of Bogue on the Moniaive road, at its junction with the road to Lochinvar. As the picture suggests, both mill and miller's house were very old. The house was one of the last in Galloway to have its fire in the centre of the floor, using an old millstone as hearth. It then progressed to a gable chimney of clay and straw, perhaps a 'hingin lum', before acquiring the more conventional chimneys shown here. It has been suggested that Gordieston, as it was known locally, was the location of Viscount Kenmure's unsuccessful first attempt to found a royal burgh in 1629. His second attempt the following year fared rather better, resulting in the town of New Galloway.

The transformation of the Deugh–Ken river system by the hydroelectric project of the 1930s was less total north of the Carsphairn Lane watercourse, which brought water down from the northern part of the catchment area. Here, in contrast to further south, the level of the Deugh was lowered, since only enough water to keep the river flowing came down this way. Hence the precarious perches occupied by Carsphairn's version of 'The Last of the Summer Wine' would be available to succeeding generations. The attraction of this scene was appreciated by the artist James Paterson of Moniaive, one of the famous Glasgow Boys group. He painted it, but without its human element. The lady in the upper right-hand corner looks understandably apprehensive.

The Deugh and Ken were very popular with anglers both for the quality of the salmon and trout fishing and for the magnificent scenery. Here, below the Carsphairn Lane, the huge increase in volume of water that resulted from the power scheme becoming operational raised the river level by many feet, submerging much of what is visible in the photograph and totally altering the view. Even in monochrome it is possible to see how the Deugh earned its Gaelic name 'The Black Water'.

The Tinkler's Loup was one of the best known spots on the pre-1930s Deugh and the scene of a traditional tale. According to this a tinker named Clement, being pursued for a theft but thinking he had outdistanced his pursuers, lay down to rest at the side of the gorge only to be surprised by them. Pausing long enough to collect his booty, he leapt nimbly across the 16' 4" chasm and, with no one willing to attempt to repeat his feat, made a leisurely escape.

Tinkler's Loup, Galloway.

NEW BRIDGE AT TINKERS LOUP DAM, CARSPHAIRN, KIRKCUDBRIGHTSHIRE.   A.9235.

The spectacular rise in the level of the Deugh and the effect on the landscape brought about by the electricity scheme are obvious from this post-1936 view of the Tinkler's Loup. It is little wonder that the author of *Highways and Byways* expressed himself on the subject with unusual force for such a mild-mannered man: 'Perhaps a time will come when . . . people . . . will say that in such places such works shall no longer be permitted merely because water happens to be cheaper than coal.'

Kendoon Power Station, Galloway.

Kendoon is the most northerly of the five power stations comprising the Galloway scheme. The surge tower in the centre of the picture is intended to protect the station's pipes and turbines by absorbing sudden variations in water pressure. In the middle ground are the bungalows of Kendoon village, built by the Galloway Water Power Company for its workers but later surplus to requirements and some years ago offered for sale as a single lot. C. H. Dick was critical of the village name, saying it should have properly been called Dundeugh, but accepting that the pronunciation of this form might have created problems for southern tongues. Kendoon can produce 1,100 kW of electricity within five minutes of start-up.

Below the meeting of the Deugh and Ken the combined river adopts the latter name, an inevitable step since the Gaelic *ceann* means 'head' or 'chief'. The Ken, illustrated here, formerly exhibited the same characteristics as higher up the valley, with rocky gorges and heavily wooded landscapes justifying the description of this area as the Galloway or Southern Highlands. The picture well illustrates 'the many beautiful windings' of the river commented on by the Dalry minister as far back as 1791.

Carsfad Dam, Galloway.

Carsfad dam and its attendant buildings seem raw and obtrusive in the landscape here in the scheme's early days. Awareness of the impact on a famously beautiful area led to the appointment by the Scottish Office of a Scenery Committee to advise the promoters. One of its recommendations was that local whinstone or granite should be used in the concrete mixes and as much as possible in the buildings. Many people would agree that today the harsh lines have softened and the buildings and dams are no longer so prominent in the environment. Carsfad dam and power station were second in the chain from north to south.

Writers of the earlier twentieth century rhapsodise about the dramatic scenery of Earlstoun Linn, where spawning salmon attempted to fight their way upriver against a ferocious current. Very few stretches of the river have survived unscathed and this is not one of them: apart from a few inches of the highest rocks, everything is now submerged.

The Galloway Water Power Company was anxious to avoid opposition to its plans from the influential owners of fishing rights on the upper Ken. It therefore went to great lengths to try to ensure that spawning salmon would continue to have access to the upper reaches. To this end fish ladders were constructed at the Tongland, Earlstoun, and Carsfad dams. These were scientifically designed after much research and experiment and based on successful versions on the River Shannon. The ladders consist of a series of chambers with a rise of two feet between them and resting pools every 20 feet of vertical height. Communication between adjacent chambers is by submerged openings, which are adjustable so that changes in the amount of water flowing down the ladder do not affect the water level in each chamber. Here at Earlstoun the ladder is 70½ feet high, making it one of the highest ever constructed up until that time.

GALLOWAY HYDRO ELECTRIC POWER WORKS. EARLSTOUN POWER STATION AND FISH LADDER UNDER CONSTRUCTION.

Earlstoun is the most southerly in the chain of three power stations in the Ken–Deugh valley. Like its two neighbours to the north it is operated remotely from Glenlee station. Milton Park, built in the early nineteenth century and later much extended, can just be seen among the trees in the right middle ground. The name (mill toun) indicates that several hundred years before the building of the power station, the waters of the Ken were already being harnessed to drive machinery, in this case almost certainly that of a corn mill. Milton Park seems to have been built by Alexander Kennedy on land that was previously part of Earlstoun estate. It is now a hotel.

EARLSTOUN DAM, NEAR CARSPHAIRN, KIRKCUDBRIGHTSHIRE

A5851.

Earlstoun is an arch-and-gravity dam with its wall sharply curved to resist the thrust of the water. It is over 60 feet high and more than 600 feet long. The reservoir is about 130 acres in extent. In an imaginative move, the power company commissioned well-known Kirkcudbright artist Charles Oppenheimer to execute paintings of dams under construction. One of the results was on show at the Homecoming exhibition in Kirkcudbright in 2000.

GLENLEE ELECTRIC POWER STATION, NEW GALLOWAY.

A.2154.

Glenlee power station is situated north-west of New Galloway and powered by water from artificial Clatteringshaws Loch, which is brought to it by tunnel and pipeline, the latter clearly visible here. The tunnel, 3½ miles long, 11½ feet in diameter, and concrete-lined, was the biggest construction job in the entire hydroelectric scheme. It was excavated simultaneously from six faces at a rate of 100 feet per week. Glenlee and Kendoon are the only stations in the scheme which use water which has not already passed through another power station.

Pipe Line and Power Station, Glenlee.
New Galloway.

The impressive Glenlee pipeline is over a quarter of a mile long with a diameter of approximately eight feet. Its steep gradient creates a head of water which gives Glenlee a power output second only to Tongland. In the middle ground are the pylons carrying the electricity to the national grid. It was the construction of the latter in 1926 which made the Galloway Water Power Scheme feasible by providing a market for its electricity. The River Ken can be seen to the right with Dalry village beyond. The hay crop from the river meadows has been cut and put into stacks.

CLATTERINGSHAWS DAM, NEW GALLOWAY, KIRKCUDBRIGHTSHIRE   A.2123 (W)

The creation of the reservoir at Clatteringshaws radically altered the landscape. The Black Water of Dee was dammed in a marshy area and a loch of 1,000 acres created. From the east it seems natural but an approach from the west reveals the truth, as shown here. At 500 yards the dam is the second longest in the scheme. Its presence necessitated a change in the line of the public road and this in turn led to the replacement of the Upper Bridge of Dee by the new structure in the picture. Through its arches those of its predecessor can just be glimpsed a few yards upstream. The earliest bridge of all over the Black Water is some distance away submerged under the loch. Remarkably, it was built in 1703 with the proceeds raised in a house-to-house collection throughout Galloway by a religious body, the Synod of Galloway – the Privy Council (the Scottish Executive of its day) having refused funding.

CLATTERINGSHAWS DAM.
(GALLOWAY ELECTRICAL SCHEME)

A. 2138.

The gentle curve of the Clatteringshaws dam shows it to be a gravity structure, relying on its own weight for stability. Originally the parapet walkway was open to the public but it was closed for security reasons at the start of World War Two. Perhaps wisely, it has not reopened. In the left background the outflow tower marking the start of the tunnel, which runs through the hills behind to Glenlee, can just be seen. Under the loch waters lie the Old Edinburgh Road and the remains of a homestead inhabited by a Clatteringshaws farmer 2,000 years ago. It has been partly reconstructed close to the visitor centre. The latter is itself another former farmhouse and steading, this time a mere 200 years old. Also submerged is part of Moss Raploch, scene of Bruce's 1307 victory. In the right middleground is the deep cutting that had to be blasted for the realigned road when the dam was built.